I dedicate this book to
Sherry Launt and **Vickey Barwick**.
They were the co-founders of Child and
Family Development, where I have had the
honor of working for the past 30 years.
Vickey and Sherry were amazing role models
for me. They nurtured and protected me while
encouraging my skills. They prized creativity
and excellence. I was blessed to have
ended up on their doorstep.
Thank you.

Introduction

Does your child have a friend, family member, or classmate who has Attention Deficit Hyperactivity Disorder (ADHD)? Would you like your child or the children in your classroom to understand more about ADHD? Are you looking for an engaging way to start a dialogue about ADHD? I wrote this book to help solve these challenges.

A is for ADHD is a children's picture book in an ABC format. With delightful illustrations, this book teaches traits that are not uncommon in people with ADHD. A child with ADHD narrates this book from his (or her) point of view.

As with my book, *C is for Cerebral Palsy*, I deliberately focused on a child with more significant challenges due to ADHD. Every child with ADHD has unique strengths, talents, and challenges that are likely very different from those of the child in this book. Most children with ADHD do not present with this level of challenge. This child has hyperactivity. I could have chosen a child with the inattentive type of ADHD, which is also common but has an entirely different presentation. I wanted this book to be from the point of view of a single child. In no way do I desire to negate the experience of a child who has the inattentive type. That would simply be a different book.

I hope *A is for ADHD* provides an entertaining way to start a simple educational discussion about ADHD. I invite you to read this story interactively with your child. You can discuss the choices this child makes in this book. You can talk about the consequences of his or her actions and what might have been the wiser choice. Encourage discussions of how you or people you love might be like the child in this book. You might compare and contrast how the child in this book is similar or different from a person you know with ADHD. This book provides essential opportunities to discuss how to be a friend of a child with ADHD.

As a pediatric physical therapist, I work with children who have ADHD. Others often misunderstand the actions and behaviors of people with ADHD. I believe knowledge helps break down barriers and encourages kindness and patience. Assisting children to understand ADHD at a young age is powerful. Reading this book has the potential to change your child's perceptions of ADHD. I also hope that we can help people with ADHD see all the things they do well, the unique perspectives that their differences bring, and how they can use those talents to accomplish great things.

A is for Attention Deficit Hyperactivity Disorder

A Child's View

Published by Gotcha Apps, LLC
1904 ½ Williams St.
Valdosta, GA 31602

This book provides general information on ADHD. It should not be relied upon as recommending or promoting any specific diagnosis or method of treatment. It is not intended as a substitute for medical advice or direct diagnosis and treatment of ADHD by a qualified physician. Readers who have questions about ADHD or its treatment should consult with a physician or other qualified health care professional.

ISBN:978-0-9981567-7-4

Cover art and interior artwork by Ikos Ronzkie

Text by Amy E. Sturkey, PT

A is for Attention Deficit Hyperactivity Disorder

A Child's View

written by
Amy E. Sturkey, PT

illustrated by
Ikos Ronzkie

A is for
Attention Deficit Hyperactivity Disorder.
I have ADHD. My thoughts bounce from
one thing to the next. Do you like ice cream?
My feet stink. I have a hat.
Do you like swimming?
Oh, hi!

B is for Bored.

I am never bored with video games or things that I love.
BUT I get bored of everything else long before you do.
I wish I could pay attention to the boring stuff
like you can. Next page, please!

C is for Could.
When I have a problem, I could stop, think, and ask for help. But often, I don't. Sometimes, this gets me into trouble or danger. I am working on training my brain to put on the brakes and think before acting.

D is for Distraction.

What was that? Oh, sorry! I am distracted by everything new, fun, or tricky. You can quickly pay attention to the most important things. I am working hard on learning to act before it becomes close to an emergency.

E is for Emotions.
My emotions can be all over the place.
I am learning to take time to think about how
I feel so that I do not overreact. I can be very
caring and a great friend.

F is for Focus.

I can focus better than most people on cool games that interest me, but it is so hard to focus on my schoolwork. Mom says focus is what allows you to start something and stay with it until you are finished. It is easier for you to stay on track and not get discouraged. I have trouble just getting started. Now, what was I doing?

G is for Grades.
Grades do not show everything you know.
Earning good grades was so hard until I got help.
Now I get to sit up close to the teacher,
so I can show off what I know.
I am allowed extra time on tests.
I get one-on-one tutoring at school and cognitive
behavioral therapy after school. My grades are
already getting better!

H is for Hyperactivity.
It used to feel like I had the energy to change the world, but the focus to do nothing. My extra energy truly makes it tough for me to sit still, stay in my seat, and be quiet like you. With help, I am learning to train my extra energy to blast through the work I need to get done.

I is for Impulsivity.
I can be very impulsive. If there is
something I want to do, I do it! It is hard
to stop myself even when I know
it is wrong. As I learn to slow down,
I am making better choices.

J is for Just.

My homework used to seem just impossible.
I used to forget my books and lose my homework.
Now my teacher and my parents have a plan to help
keep me organized. My mother breaks down my work
into smaller parts so I can be successful.
That helps a lot!

K is for Knowing.
Often I know what the safer and wiser choice is. I just get lost thinking about how fun and exciting the other choices are. The next thing I know, down the stairs I go.

L is for...

Huh? What? Are you talking to me?
You have asked me five times what L stands for?
It is hard to listen when there are so many exciting
things that grab my attention. L is for Listening.

M is for Medication.

Some kids need glasses to see. Some kids need wheelchairs to move. I need medication to help me pay attention, do my work, and remember important things. I just started taking medication, and I see changes already! Not every kid with ADHD needs medication, but it sure helps me!

N is for what I Need.
To do my best, Mom says that I need to eat healthy foods and get plenty of sleep. Dad makes sure I play hard for at least an hour every day. Mom helps me limit my screen time.

O is for Original.
I have lots of original and creative thoughts
that others do not have. My imagination
is my superpower!

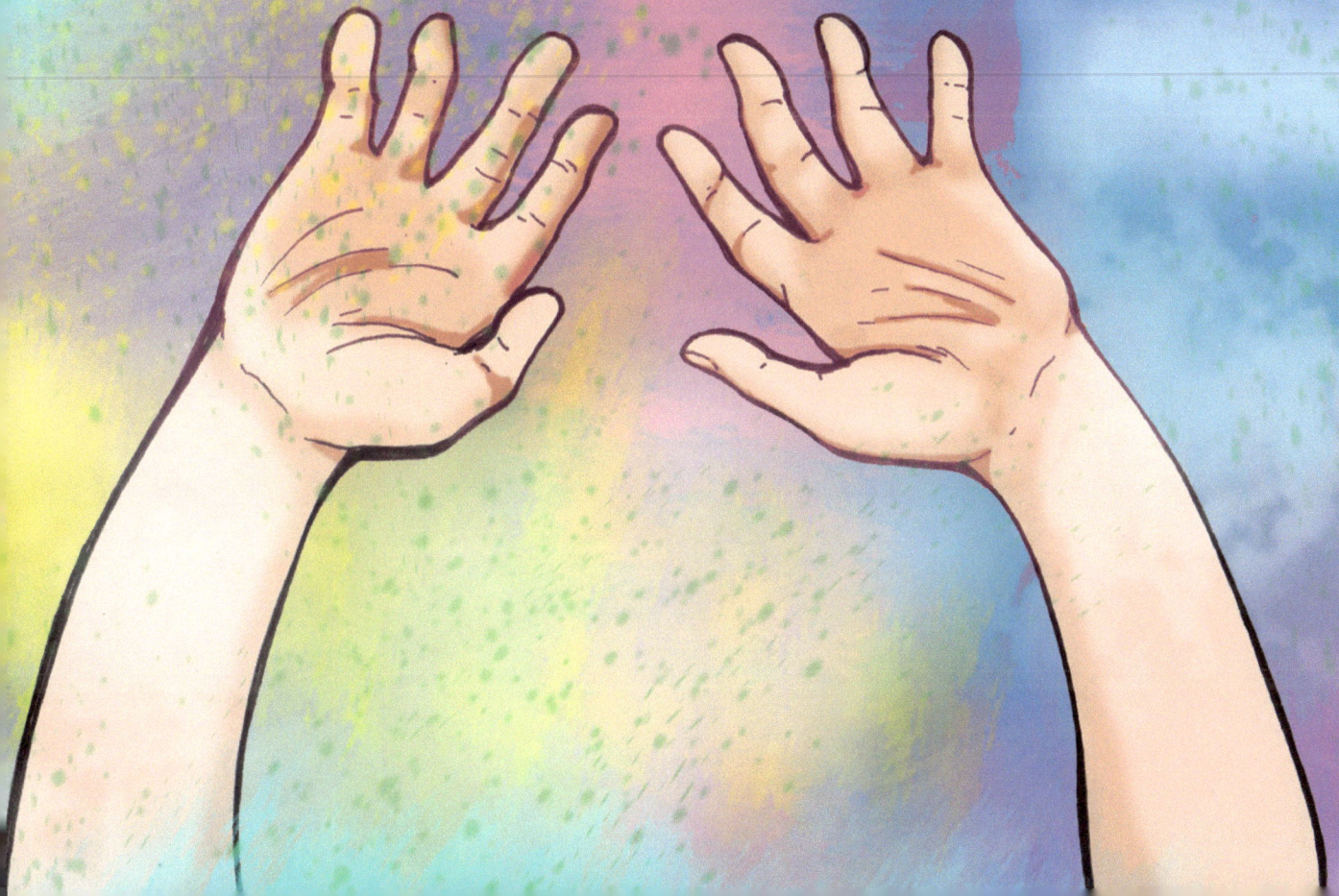

P is for Parents.
My Dad has ADHD too. Mom loves us both for who we are. Dad passed it down to me. Boys are more likely to have ADHD than girls.

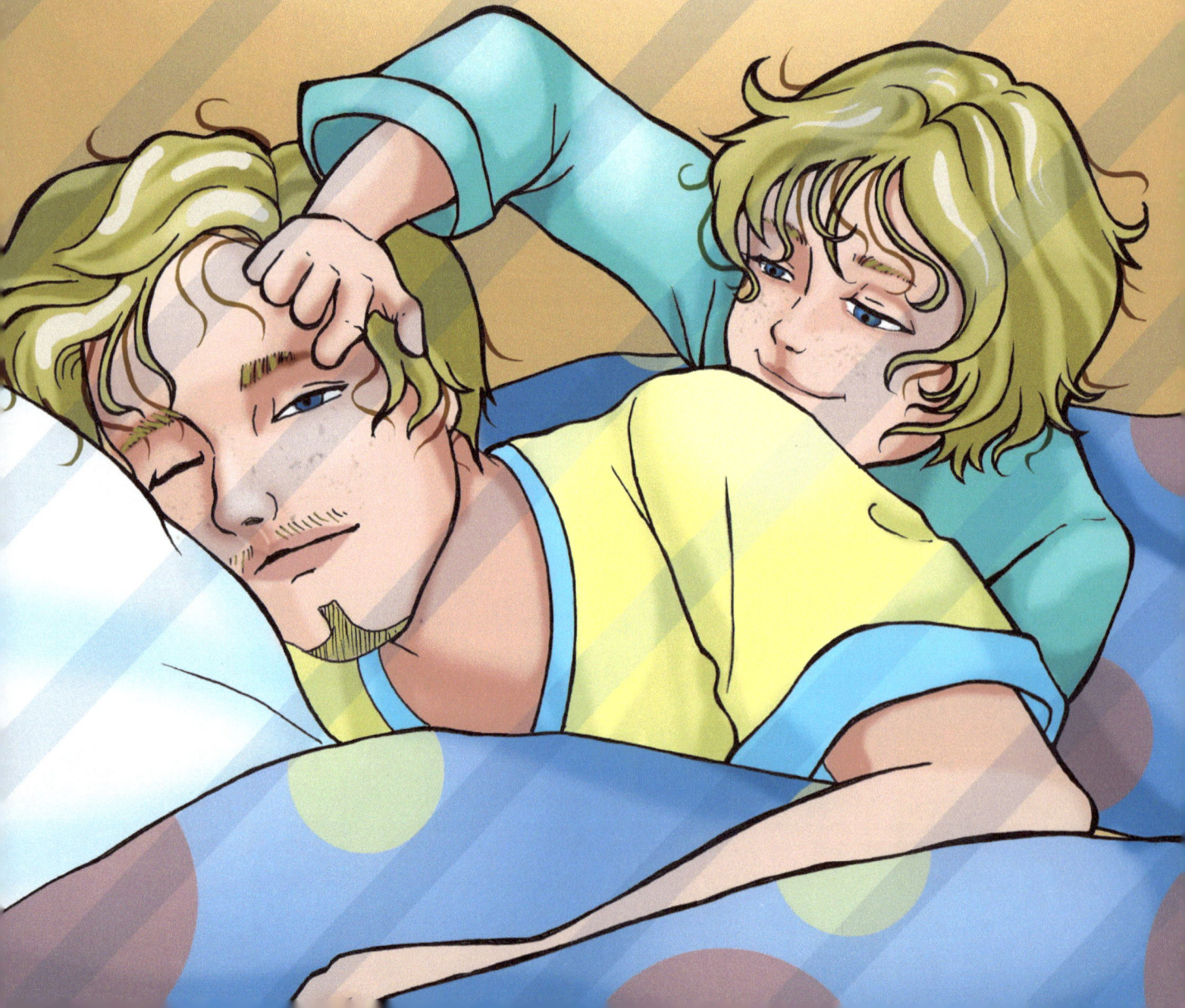

Q is for Quitting.

If something is exciting and fun to me, my mom cannot get me to quit. But when things get hard or boring, I am not very patient. Can we skip the rest of this book and go to the end now?

QUIT

R is for Routines and Rules.
They used to be enemy #1.
Now I know that rules help
me stay safe and in control.
Routines help me understand
what to expect. I would be
lost without them!

S is for Self-Control.
Dad told me that self-control is when you manage your thoughts, feelings, and actions to get more of what you want and less of what you do not want. I did not have a clue what he was talking about. Now I am learning self-control with meditation! I am learning to be the boss of my brain!

T is for Thoughts.
Sometimes I cannot stop my thoughts from zooming around in my head like a race car. I think I have more thoughts before I get out of bed than you have all day. But this can be great! Some of my ideas are awesome!

$13 \times 1 = 13$

$13 \times 2 = 26$

$13 \times 3 = 39$

$13 \times 4 = 52$

$13 \times 5 = 65$

$13 \times 6 = 78$

$13 \times 7 = 91$

$13 \times 8 = 104$

$13 \times 9 = 117$

$13 \times 10 = 130$

$13 \times 11 = 143$

$13 \times 12 = 156$

U is for Understanding.

I used to feel I wasn't as smart as my friends. Then my teacher helped me understand that my ADHD makes it hard for me to learn the same way as others. I can be just as smart as you, but I learn differently.

SUCCESS

SMARTNESS

BRIGHT FUTURE

V is for Very.
I can have a very tough
time thinking about what
other people want and need.
It can be hard for me to wait
for my turn, so I may interrupt
a lot. I am so much better at
"Follow the Leader" if I am the
boss! Can't I just be in charge?

W is for What.
As in, "What was I thinking?" I used to
take chances. I didn't think it through before
I did something risky. Now I am learning to
think about the consequences before I act.

X is for eXtra.
With my extra creativity, extra fast thinking, and extra energy, I can imagine extra creative ways to find extra trouble. Please be patient with me. I am worth it! I am growing, changing, and learning every day. Thank you for staying by my side.

Y is for You.
I am so glad you know more about ADHD now.
Everybody is different. We all need help sometimes.
With my teachers, parents, therapist, and you on my
team, I know I can do anything when I focus this
brain of mine!

Z is for Zip.
Don't mind me while I zip ahead to my fantastic life.
Lots of people with ADHD have done great things.
I can too!

The End

Consider these three requests from a child with ADHD:

3-Step Action Plan

1. Be Patient and Understanding

2. Help me Make Good Choices

3. Help me Stay on Task

Other offerings by the author:

◇◇◇◇◇◇◇◇◇◇◇◇◇◇◇◇◇◇◇◇◇◇

A is for Autism: A Child's View

D is for Down Syndrome: A Child's View

C is For Cerebral Palsy: A Child's View

Pediatric Physical Therapy Strengthening Exercises for the Hips

Pediatric Physical Therapy Strengthening Exercises for the Knees

Pediatric Physical Therapy Strengthening Exercises for the Ankle

Blog:
www.pediatricPTexercises.com

YouTube Channel:
Pediatric Physical Therapy Exercises

Facebook page:
Pediatric Physical Therapy Exercise

Pinterest page:
amysturkey/pediatric-physical-therapy

Ikos Ronzkie is an international graphic designer, book illustrator, and comic strip artist. She creates fanciful illustrations for advertisements, campaigns, comic books, character designs, book designs, and book covers. She has worked as an illustrator with local and international clientele for over 15 years.

She illustrated this author's previous three books, *A is for Autism, D is for Down Syndrome,* and *C is for Cerebral Palsy.*

She is also the illustrator for books, including: *What Babies Do, Oh, Livvie!, What Do I Do Well, The Loosey Goosey Tooth, Princess Superhero Antonia, The Tooth Fairy, What Does Alex See, A Tea for Queen Bee, My Daddy's Hat, My Mommy's Shoes, The Little Green Boat, Follow the Breadcrumbs, The Fastest Kid in the World, Silly Billy and the Magic Hut, The Land of the Dinosaurs, Willy Nilly Pokemon Hunt* and hundreds of illustrated stories.

Her clients include international publishers, dollmakers, comic book writers, authors, and picture book writers. She produces "Bayan ng Biyahero Comics" for the Antipolo Star Newspaper for the Rizal and Metro Manila distribution areas. She previously created "Estudyante Blues" for the Living News and Good Education magazine and illustrated comics for Free Fiction House Foundation. Independently, she writes and produces her own comics: "Karit," "Dalawang Liham," and "Sulsi." She is now busy with her next book anthology.

Ikos Ronzkie is the co-founder of IKOS Studios, which strives to promote and explore Philippine culture with visual and literary arts. Their creations are dedicated to work inspired by the Philippine history, myths and legends.

www.ingramcontent.com/pod-product-compliance
Lightning Source LLC
Chambersburg PA
CBHW040020050426
42452CB00002B/61